Mixes For
Cocoas,
Teas,
and
Cappuccinos

Drink Mixes Layered In Jars For Gifts

Jackie Gannaway

Published in Austin, TX by COOKBOOK CUPBOARD,
P.O. Box 50053, Austin, TX 78763
(512) 477-7070 phone (512) 891-0094 fax

ISBN 0-885597-28-2

NOTICE: The information contained in this book is true,
complete, and accurate to the best of my knowledge.
All recommendations and suggestions are made without
any guaranty on the part of the editor or Cookbook Cupboard. The editor and publisher disclaim any liability
incurred in connection with the use of this information.

Cover Design by Ann Moon

This book is
part of the
Layers of Love™
Collection from
Cookbook Cupboard.
All rights reserved.

Mail Order Information
To order a copy of this book send a check for $3.95 + $1.50
for shipping. (TX residents add 8.25 % sales tax) to Cookbook
Cupboard, P.O. Box 50053, Austin, TX 78763. Send a note
asking for this title by name. If you would like a descriptive
list of all the fun titles in The Kitchen Crafts Collection and
the Layers of Love™ Collection send or fax a note asking for
a brochure. Other books you might enjoy are "Cookies in a
Jar" (layered cookie mixes), "Gift Mixes" (assorted mixes -11
of which are layered in jars), and "Layered Soup Mixes in
Jars". All the Kitchen Crafts and Layers of Love™ titles are
$3.95. There is only one shipping charge of $1.50 per order,
not per book.

Layered Drink Mixes in Jars - Introduction

This book is full of drink mixes for you to layer in pint or quart jars (one is even in a gallon jar!). These are great to give as gifts and to sell at fund raisers and bazaars. They are inexpensive to make.

Many of the ingredients can be bought in bulk - your grocery store will have very large boxes of dry milk and 2 lb. jars of coffee creamer. Warehouse stores have really large containers (usually less expensive).

These mixes are fresh for about 6 months. Put an "expiration date" - "Please enjoy this cocoa mix by April 1, 2001" for example.

There is a complete list of all the recipes on pg. 32.

The recipes in this book give you:

1) - a list of ingredients for the jar.
2) - the order in which to place ingredients in jar.
3) - instructions for you to copy to attach to the jar.

What Kind Of Jars To Use

These recipes call for either pint or quart jars. Wide mouth canning jars work best because you can get your fingers inside. These jars are sold in cases of 12 at grocery stores, hardware stores and discount stores.

Regular canning jars (not wide mouth) will also work as will mayonnaise jars. If you are using food jars (such as spaghetti sauce jars) be very sure they are a true pint (16 oz. or 2 cups) or a true quart (32 oz. or 4 cups). Food companies are making jars smaller every year.

The 11 oz. clear glass jars containing instant tea hold a little bit more than 1 quart - use them for some of the quart size drink mix recipes. (Don't be confused by the fact that the tea jar is 11 oz. - in this case it is a measurement of weight of the dry tea powder not the volume of 32 oz. of liquid.)

Look For Other Fun Jars

Import stores have several alternative jars. There is a squarish glass jar with a clamp down lid. It comes in

1 liter and 500 milliliter size. Use the 1 liter in place of the quart jar in these recipes and use the 500 milliliter (which is a half liter) for the pint recipes (you will have to add a very few more ingredients or more marsh-mallows or a crushed piece of aluminum foil to completely fill these jars, but that won't effect the recipe).

These jars cost $3.00 to $6.00 each as compared to 65¢ to 75¢ for the canning jars, so think about your budget.

How To Decorate The Jars

1) Cover lid with a circle of fabric. Hold in place with a rubber band -tie on a ribbon or raffia bow. Hot glue a small amount of fiberfill under the fabric for a "puffy" look.

2) Tape flat lid onto the jar and place a circle of fabric over that. Screw on the ring to hold fabric in place.

3) Fabric is available to match any theme. Go to a fabric store and be amazed at the styles - every holiday fabric, dice fabrics for Bunko prizes, playing card fabrics for bridge prizes, school fabric for teachers.

4) Cross stitch or appliqué the fabric for the lid.

5) Use wrapping paper or brown paper sack instead of fabric (rubber stamp on the brown paper sack).

6) Coordinate the fabric with the colors in the mix.

7) Paint a design on the jar with paint for glass - or even a make it look like a stained glass or etched glass jar with the products available at crafts stores.

How To Write The Instructions

1) Copy instructions onto a recipe card and attach.

2) Type instructions into your computer. Add graphics, use a color printer (or colored paper).

3) Rubber stamp the recipe card with fun designs.

4) Add stickers to the recipe card.

How To Make A "Sand-Art" Design

When you have completed layering the ingredients take a plain table knife or a skewer and push it to the bottom of the jar at the edge, touching the glass. Pull knife up against the glass. Some of the mix will rise up making a pointed design. Repeat this around the entire jar. You can alternate pushing down with pulling up or you can just pull up.

It is easier to do this before adding the last layer. Often this causes the mix to settle a little so you may have to add a little more of the last ingredient to completely fill the jar. This won't effect the recipe.

If the last ingredient is a bag of marshmallows, just add a few more marshmallows to the bag to fill the jar.

If the recipe calls for a paper circle, you can still make a sand art design with the ingredients from the paper circle up to the top of the jar.

How To Make A Diagonal Design

Decide on this design before putting any ingredients into the jar. Have each ingredient ready in small containers. Have a small scoop ready to use in filling the jar.

Hold the empty jar in one hand at a severe slant (like a 45° angle). With the other hand, using the scoop if necessary, add the first layer. Keeping the jar on a slant, add the rest of the ingredients in order. Place the jar on the counter and press down the last ingredient, adding a little more if necessary to fill the jar. The slanted layers will stay in place for a very interesting look.

If the recipe calls for a paper circle, it can be added on a slant and this design will still work.

Have Fun!

Have fun with these recipes in this book. Don't worry about the very exact proportions, sometimes a Tb. or two here or there will be necessary due to settling as you add the ingredients. I think you will enjoy the flavor variety in these recipes as well as the color variety (they are not all cocoa brown!).

Double Chocolate Cocoa Mix in a Quart Jar

Ingredients for Jar

2/3 cup powdered coffee creamer

2/3 cup milk chocolate chips (not semi-sweet, but <u>milk chocolate</u> chips)

circle of heavy paper

2/3 cup powdered sugar

2/3 cup chocolate flavored drink mix (like Quik®)

2/3 cup dry milk

1 1/3 cups mini marshmallows in a zipper sandwich bag

Size of Jar: Quart

Place Ingredients in Jar in This Order:

(If you want to make a diagonal design read pg. 5 before putting ingredients in jar.)

1. Place ingredients in order listed above, placing a circle of heavy paper on top of chips to prevent powdered sugar from sifting down through the chips. Then add remaining ingredients.
2. Place bag of marshmallows in jar last.
3. Decorate jar (pg. 4).
4. Attach recipe below to jar.

 Double Chocolate Cocoa

1. Remove marshmallows from jar. Set aside.
2. Empty cocoa mix into a large mixing bowl. Remove and discard paper circle.
3. Blend mix very well with a whisk.
4. Place mix back into jar or a container of your choice.
5. Place 1 1/2 to 2 Tb. mix into a cup. Add 1 cup boiling water. Stir until mixture is completely dissolved. Top with marshmallows.

Americana Double Chocolate Cocoa Mix

Make Double Chocolate Cocoa Mix on pg. 6, but put 1 (1.75 oz.) bottle Betty Crocker Decor All American Colors® (red, white and blue soft sprinkles) into jar first. Don't confuse these with hard round sprinkles - these are soft and chewy.
At holiday time these sprinkles are available in Christmas and Halloween colors.
Add fewer marshmallows - the sprinkles take up extra room, leaving less room for marshmallows.

Cocoa Flavoring in a Tiny Jar

Mix the next 4 ingredients in small bowl:

1 tsp. cinnamon
1/2 tsp. nutmeg
1 Tb. powdered sugar
1 1/2 Tb. powdered coffee creamer

1/4 cup milk chocolate chips, (not semi-sweet, but <u>milk chocolate</u>)
1/4 cup vanilla chips (like chocolate chips, but vanilla)

Size of Jar: 1/2 cup
This is 4 oz. - like a baby food jar.
(A "tall" baby food jar - like a juice jar - works well.)

Place Ingredients in Jar in This Order:

1. Place spice mixture in jar first.
2. Place half the chocolate chips in jar next.
3. Place all the vanilla chips in jar.
4. Add remaining chocolate chips, pressing in firmly.
5. Attach these instructions:
   1) Empty mix into a bowl - mix well. Place mix into a small plastic container to store.
   2. Stir 1 heaping tsp. into hot cocoa or 1 heaping Tb. into hot coffee. Stir well to melt chips.

Marshmallow Cocoa Mix in a Quart Jar

Ingredients for Jar

Mix next two ingredients in small bowl:
1/4 cup powdered coffee creamer
1/2 cup powdered sugar

1/3 cup cocoa powder

Mix next three ingredients in small bowl:
1/2 cup sugar
1 1/2 cups dry milk
1/4 tsp. salt

1 cup mini marshmallows in a small zipper
sandwich bag

Size of Jar: Quart

Place Ingredients in Jar in This Order:

(If you want to make a diagonal design read pg. 5
before putting ingredients in jar.)

1. Place creamer mixture in jar first.
2. Place cocoa powder in jar next, spreading evenly to
   edges of jar.
3. Place dry milk mixture into jar next.
4. Leave layered as is or make a "Sand-Art" design (pg. 5).
5. Place bag of mini marshmallows in jar last.
6. Decorate jar (pg. 4).
7. Attach recipe on pg. 9 to jar.

This recipe continued from pg. 8.

Marshmallow Cocoa

1. Remove marshmallows from jar. Set aside.
2. Empty cocoa mix into a large mixing bowl.
3. Blend very well with a whisk.
4. Place mix back into jar or a container of your choice.
5. Place 2 heaping Tb. mix into a cup. Add 1 cup water. Stir until mixture is completely dissolved. Top with mini marshmallows.

Chocolate Milkshake

1. Place 1 scoop soft vanilla ice cream and 1 cup milk into a quart jar.
2. Add 2 Tb. Cocoa Mix.
3. Place lid on jar and shake until blended (or blend in blender).

Chocolate Milk

1. Place 1 cup milk into a glass.
2. Add 2 heaping Tb. Cocoa Mix. Stir to blend.

Feathers and Butterflies!

Walk through a craft store or the craft section at Wal-Mart and find many things that can be hot glued on top of the fabric on top of the jar of mix. I particularly like Wal-Mart because it has fabrics and crafts in the same part of the store. You can choose a small bird made of feathers or a silk butterfly and then choose a fabric and ribbon that coordinates with it.

You will get many jar decorating ideas this way that may not have otherwise come to you.

They will also have a variety of seasonal decorations for whatever the occasion.

Colorado Cocoa Mix in a Gallon Jar
(Everything is bigger in the West!)

Ingredients for Jar

1 (8 qt. size) box dry milk
1 (11 oz.) jar powdered creamer
1 cup powdered sugar
1 tsp. salt (optional)
2 (1 lb.) boxes chocolate flavored drink mix (like Quik®)

1. Mix milk, creamer, sugar and salt in large pan. Remove approx. half this mixture and place in another dish. You now have 2 dishes with white mixture in them.
2. Add 1 box of chocolate drink mix to one of the white mixtures. You now have 1 dish with white mixture, 1 dish with a pale chocolate mixture and 1 unopened box of chocolate drink mix. This gives you 3 colors to layer.

Size of Jar: Gallon! Yes, a gallon, really.

Place Ingredients in Jar in This Order:

1. Place half the white mixture in jar first.
2. Place half the new box of chocolate drink mix in jar next. Spread it evenly and press down firmly.
3. Place all the pale chocolate mixture in jar next.
4. Place remaining chocolate drink mix from box in jar. Spread it evenly and press down firmly.
5. Place remaining white mixture in jar last.
   You will have 5 layers: white, dark chocolate, pale chocolate, dark chocolate and white.

Recipe continued on pg. 11.

This recipe continued from pg. 10.

6. Leave layered as is or make a "Sand-Art" design (pg. 5).
7. Decorate jar (pg. 4).
8. Attach recipe below to jar.

Cocoa

1. Empty Cocoa Mix into a large pan.
2. Blend mix together very well with a whisk.
3. Place mix back into jar or a container of your choice.
4. Place 3 Tb. mix into a cup. Add 1 cup boiling water.
   Stir until mixture is completely dissolved.
   Top with whipped cream if desired.

Where To Get Gallon Jars

Get gallon jars from restaurants, concession stands, school cafeteria after they are through with them. Buy them with pickles, mustard or mayonnaise in them. Glass or clear plastic jars will work.

Buy nice gallon jars at import stores. Import stores will also have 4 liter jars. If you use a 4 liter jar, put a bag of mini marshmallows in the top of the jar to fill up the extra space.

A Spoonful of Luxury

Tie a freshly polished silverplate spoon to a jar of mix with some ribbon or raffia.

Mismatched silverplate spoons sell for 50¢ to $3.00 each at flea markets and at antiques stores.

Orange Cocoa Mix in a Pint Jar

Ingredients for Jar

1/3 cup powdered orange flavored drink mix

3/4 cup powdered coffee creamer

1/2 cup chocolate flavored drink mix (like Quik®)

1/2 cup powdered sugar

Size of Jar: Pint

Place Ingredients in Jar in This Order:

(If you want to make a diagonal design read pg. 5 before putting ingredients in jar.)

1. Place ingredients in jar in order listed above.
2. Leave layered as is or make a "Sand-Art" design (pg. 5).
3. Decorate jar (pg. 4).
4. Attach recipe below to jar.

 ## Orange Cocoa

1. Empty cocoa mix into a large mixing bowl.
2. Blend very well with a whisk.
3. Place mix back into jar or a container of your choice.
4. Place 1 1/2 to 2 Tb. mix into a cup. Add 1 cup boiling water. Stir until mixture is completely dissolved. Top with whipped cream if desired.

Orange Chocolate Milkshake

1. Place 1 scoop soft vanilla ice cream and 1 cup milk into a quart jar.
2. Add 2 Tb. Orange Cocoa Mix.
3. Place lid on jar and shake until blended (or blend in a blender).

Flavored Cocoa Mix in a Pint Jar

Flavors: Amaretto, Hazelnut, Vanilla, Irish Creme

Ingredients for Jar

Mix following 3 ingredients in a small bowl:

1/2 cup powdered sugar
1/2 cup + 2 Tb. flavored* powdered coffee creamer
1/2 cup dry milk

1/2 cup chocolate flavored drink mix (like Quik®)

*Powdered coffee creamer is available in several flavors.
Try: amaretto, hazelnut, vanilla and Irish creme.

Size of Jar: Pint

Place Ingredients in Jar in This Order:

(If you want to make a diagonal design read pg. 5 before putting ingredients in jar.)

1. Place half the milk mixture into jar.
2. Place half the chocolate drink mix in jar next.
3. Add the remaining milk mixture.
4. Add the remaining chocolate drink mix.
5. Leave layered as is or make a "Sand-Art" design (pg. 5).
6. Decorate jar (pg. 4).
7. Attach recipe below to jar. Name cocoa by flavor.

 _____Cocoa

1. Empty cocoa mix into a large mixing bowl.
2. Blend very well with a whisk.
3. Place mix back into jar or a container of your choice.
4. Place 1 1/2 to 2 Tb. mix into a cup. Add 1 cup boiling
   water. Stir until mixture is completely dissolved.
   Top with whipped cream if desired.

Make the recipe above into CINNAMON COCOA by using unflavored creamer and adding 2 tsp. cinnamon.

Peppermint Cocoa Mix in a Pint Jar

Ingredients for Jar

1/2 cup powdered coffee creamer

1 (2.25 oz.) bottle Betty Crocker Decor® or Wilton® red sugar, (in section of store with cake mixes) or color 1/3 cup sugar with a few drops red food coloring and mix well.

1/4 cup hard peppermint candy discs, crushed (in blender, food processor or by placing candy in a small plastic freezer bag and tapping lightly with a hammer)

circle of heavy paper

1/3 cup powdered sugar

1/2 cup chocolate flavored drink mix (like Quik®)

1/2 cup dry milk (scant 1/2 cup)

Size of Jar: Pint

Place Ingredients in Jar in This Order:

(If you want to make a diagonal design read pg. 5 before putting ingredients in jar.)

1. Place ingredients in order listed above, placing a circle of heavy paper on top of the crushed peppermints to prevent powdered sugar from sifting down through the peppermints.
2. Decorate jar (pg. 4).
3. Attach recipe on pg. 15 to jar.

This recipe continued from pg. 14.

Peppermint Cocoa

1. Empty cocoa mix into a large mixing bowl.
   Remove and discard paper circle.
2. Blend mix very well with a whisk.
3. Place mix back into jar or a container of your choice.
4. Place 1 1/2 to 2 Tb. mix into a cup. Add 1 cup boiling
   water. Stir until mixture is completely dissolved.
   Top with whipped cream if desired.

Cider Seasoning in a Tiny Jar

1/4 cup powdered lemonade mix

Mix next 3 ingredients together:

1/4 cup sugar
2 tsp. cinnamon mixed with
1 tsp. nutmeg

1. Layer this mix in a 4 oz. baby food jar or other
   jar that holds 1/2 cup (like a spice jar).
2. Alternate lemonade with sugar mixture.
   Make 4 layers.
3. Decorate jar (pg. 4). Attach cinnamon sticks if desired.
4. Attach instructions below:

Cider Seasoning

1. Empty contents of jar into a small bowl and blend
   well. Place mix back in jar.
2. Stir 1 tsp. Cider Simmer into 1 cup of hot apple juice,
   hot cranberry juice or hot cider.

Double this recipe to fill a one cup size jar.

Peach (or Raspberry) Tea Mix in a Pint Jar

Ingredients for Jar

2 (4 serving size) boxes peach or raspberry Jello®, (with sugar, not sugar free) (Can use 1 large box Jello®)

Mix the next two ingredients:

1/2 cup + 2 Tb. sugar

1 tsp. ginger   Note: (Peach Jello® is white in color, just like sugar. For a more interesting look, color sugar with red and yellow food coloring to make sugar a peach color.)

1/2 cup + 2 Tb. instant tea (unsweetened)

If you want PEACH MINT TEA, mix 1/2 tsp. mint extract into the sugar.

Size of Jar: Pint

Place Ingredients in Jar in This Order:

(If you want to make a diagonal design read pg. 5 before putting ingredients in jar.)

1. Empty Jello® packages into a dish. Place half this into jar first.
2. Place half the sugar in jar next, spreading evenly to edges of jar.
3. Place half the tea in jar next.
4. Repeat layers.
5. Leave layered as is or make a "Sand-Art" design (pg. 5).
6. Decorate jar (pg. 4).
7. Attach recipe on pg. 17 to jar. Name tea by flavor.

This recipe continued from pg. 16.

_____Tea - Hot

1. Empty Tea Mix into a large mixing bowl.
2. Blend very well with a whisk.
3. Place mix back into jar or a container of your choice.
4. Place 1 1/2 to 2 Tb. mix into a cup. Add 1 cup boiling water. Stir until mixture is completely dissolved.

_____ Tea - Iced

1. Place 2 Tb. mix into a glass. Add 1 cup water. Stir very well until mixture is completely dissolved. Add ice cubes.

Strawberry or Cherry* Tea Mix in a Pint Jar

Ingredients for Jar

(If you want to make a diagonal design read pg. 5 before putting ingredients in jar.)

1 cup strawberry or cherry drink mix powder

1/2 cup + 2 Tb. sugar

1/2 cup + 2 Tb. instant tea (unsweetened)

Layer in 6 parts: half drink powder, half sugar, half tea, remaining drink mix, remaining sugar, remaining tea. Leave layered as is or make a "Sand-Art" design (pg. 5).

Use instructions above for preparing tea.

*This is the same recipe as Peach or Raspberry Tea (pg. 16 and above) (without ginger or mint) except instead of using Jello® you are using powdered cherry or strawberry drink mix.

Russian Tea Mix in a Quart Jar

Ingredients for Jar

Mix the next five ingredients in a small bowl:
1 1/4 cups instant tea (unsweetened)
1 Tb. cinnamon
2 tsp. nutmeg
1 tsp. ginger
1/2 tsp. cloves (optional)

1 1/2 cups instant orange flavored breakfast drink

1 1/2 cups instant lemonade powder with sugar

cinnamon sticks (optional)

Size of Jar: Quart

Place Ingredients in Jar in This Order:
(If you want to make a diagonal design read pg. 5 before putting ingredients in jar.)

1. Place ingredients in jar in order listed above, but only do half at a time (half the tea mixture, half the orange, half the lemon, remaining tea, remaining orange, remaining lemon).
2. Leave layered as is or make a "Sand-Art" design (pg. 5).
3. Decorate jar (pg. 4). Attach cinnamon sticks if desired.
4. Attach recipe on pg. 19 to jar.

☆ ☆ ☆ ☆ ☆ ☆ ☆ ☆ ☆ ☆

Rubber Stamp Ideas

Visit a store that specializes in rubber stamps. They will be a wonderland of ideas for decorating the jars.

They have labels, kitchen stamps, coordinating stickers and many other ideas for decorating the jars.

You can add color and glitter to rubber stamps to make amazing works or art (and you don't need to be an artist).

This recipe continued from pg. 18.

Russian Tea

1. Empty mix into a large mixing bowl.
2. Blend very well with a whisk.
3. Place mix back into jar or a container of your choice.
4. Place 1 1/2 to 2 Tb. mix into a cup. Add 1 cup boiling water. Stir until mixture is completely dissolved.

Hot Buttered Rum Mix (Not In A Jar)

1 (16 oz.) box brown sugar (2 1/2 cups)
1 tsp. cinnamon
1 tsp. nutmeg

1 tsp. cloves
1/2 tsp. salt
1 stick real butter, (room temp)

1. Mix brown sugar and spices in large bowl.
2. Slice butter into 4 pieces. Mix with sugar.
   Mix well with a spoon or electric mixer.
3. Place in a plastic container with a tight lid.
   Store in refrigerator.
4. Attach instructions below:

Hot Buttered Rum

Place 1 to 2 tsp. mix in a mug. Add 1/2 to 1 jigger rum. Fill mug with boiling water.

Serve with a cinnamon stick or 1 Tb. vanilla ice cream. Mix keeps indefinitely in refrigerator.

Mulled Wine or Cider

For mulled wine or hot apple cider place 1 tsp. mix into a mug. Add 1 cup red wine or apple cider.

Heat in microwave for 1 minute. (Can simmer larger quantities on stove.)

Spiced Lemon Tea Mix in a Quart Jar

Ingredients for Jar

Mix the next 4 ingredients in a small bowl:
2 cups instant lemon tea (unsweetened but <u>with lemon</u>)
1 Tb. ginger
2 tsp. allspice
2 tsp. cloves (optional)

2 1/4 cups sugar

Size of Jar: Quart

Place Ingredients in Jar in This Order:

(If you want to make a diagonal design read pg. 5 before putting ingredients in jar.)

1. Place ingredients in jar in order listed above, but only do half at a time (half the tea mixture, half the sugar, remaining tea, remaining sugar).
2. Leave layered as is or make a "Sand-Art" design (pg. 5).
3. Decorate jar (pg. 4).
4. Attach recipe below to jar.

Spiced Lemon Tea

1. Empty mix into a large mixing bowl.
2. Blend very well with a whisk.
3. Place mix back into jar or a container of your choice.
4. Place 1 1/2 to 2 Tb. mix into a cup. Add 1 cup boiling water. Stir until mixture is completely dissolved.

Lemon Mint Iced Tea Mix in a Pint Jar

Ingredients for Jar

1/2 cup pink lemonade powder

1 (2.25 oz.) bottle Betty Crocker Decor® or Wilton® green sugar, (in section of store with cake mixes) or color 1/3 cup sugar with a few drops green food coloring and mix well.

3/4 cup lemonade powder mixed well with 1/2 tsp. mint extract

3/4 cup instant tea powder without sugar

Size of Jar: Pint

Place Ingredients in Jar in This Order:

(If you want to make a diagonal design read pg. 5 before putting ingredients in jar.)

1. Place ingredients in jar in order listed above.
2. Leave layered as is or make a "Sand-Art" design (pg. 5).
3. Decorate jar (pg. 4).
4. Attach recipe on below to jar.

Lemon Mint Iced Tea

1. Empty Lemon Tea Mix into a large mixing bowl.
2. Blend very well with a whisk.
3. Place mix back into jar or a container of your choice.
4. Place 1 1/2 to 2 Tb. mix into a cup. Add 1 cup water. Stir until mixture is completely dissolved. Add ice.

Lemon Iced Tea Mix in a Quart Jar

Ingredients for Jar

1 1/2 cups pink lemonade powder
1 1/2 cups instant tea powder (unsweetened)
1 1/2 cups lemonade powder

Size of Jar: Quart

Place Ingredients in Jar in This Order:

(If you want to make a diagonal design read pg. 5
before putting ingredients in jar.)

1. Place half the pink lemonade powder in jar first.
2. Place half the tea into jar next - press firmly.
3. Add half the lemonade next.
4. Repeat layers.
5. Leave layered as is or make a "Sand-Art" design (pg. 5).
6. Decorate jar (pg. 4).
7. Attach recipe on below to jar.

Lemon Iced Tea

1. Empty Lemon Tea Mix into a large mixing bowl.
2. Blend very well with a whisk.
3. Place mix back into jar or a container of your choice.
4. Place 1 1/2 to 2 Tb. mix into a cup. Add 1 cup water.
   Stir until mixture is completely dissolved. Add ice.

Strawberry Lemon Iced Tea

Substitute powdered strawberry drink mix for pink
lemonade in the recipe above.

Americana Vanilla Warmer Mix in a Pint Jar

Ingredients for Jar

Mix the following 5 ingredients in a small bowl:

1/4 cup sugar
1/2 cup powdered coffee creamer
1/2 cup dry milk
1/4 cup powdered sugar
2 Tb. vanilla powder (sold near the coffee creamers or in places like Starbucks that sell coffee flavorings)

1 (1.75 oz.) bottle Betty Crocker Decor® All American Colors (red, white and blue soft sprinkles) (in section of store with cake mixes). Don't confuse these with hard round sprinkles - these are soft and chewy. At holiday time they are available in Christmas and Halloween colors as well as the red, white and blue which are available year round.

Size of Jar: Pint

Place Ingredients in Jar in This Order:

(If you want to make a diagonal design read pg. 5 before putting ingredients in jar.)

1. Place half the white mixture into jar.
2. Place the red, white and blue sprinkles in jar next.
3. Fill jar with remaining white mixture.
4. Decorate jar (pg. 4).
5. Attach recipe on below to jar.

Vanilla Warmer

1. Empty mix into a bowl and mix well.
2. Place mix back into jar or a container of your choice.
3. Place 2-3 Tb. mix into a cup. Add 1 cup boiling water.

CINNAMON WARMER - Make recipe above. Place 1 Tb. cinnamon and 1 tsp. ground cloves in jar first.

Dreamsicle® Drink Mix in a Pint Jar

Ingredients for Jar

1/4 cup sugar mixed well with a few drops red and
yellow food coloring to make orange colored sugar

Mix the following 4 ingredients in a small bowl:

1/3 cup powdered coffee creamer
1/2 cup dry milk
1/4 cup powdered sugar
1/3 cup orange flavored drink mix

1 cup mini marshmallows placed in a thin zipper
sandwich bag (use the orange ones from a bag of
colored mini marshmallows and white mini
marshmallows)

Size of Jar: Pint

Place Ingredients in Jar in This Order:

(If you want to make a diagonal design read pg. 5
before putting ingredients in jar.)

1. Place orange colored sugar in jar first, pressing with
   your fingers to level.
2. Place half the milk mixture in jar next.
3. Place orange drink mix in jar next, pressing firmly.
4. Add remaining milk mixture. Press in firmly.
5. Leave layered as is or make a "Sand-Art" design (pg. 5).
6. Add bag of mini marshmallows last.
7. Decorate jar (pg. 4).
8. Attach recipe on pg. 25 to jar.

This recipe continued from pg. 24.

Dreamsicle® Warmer

1. Remove bag of marshmallows from jar. Set aside.
2. Empty mix into a bowl and mix well.
3. Place mix back into jar or a container of your choice.
4. Place 3 Tb. mix into a cup. Add 1 cup boiling water.
   Stir until mixture is completely dissolved.
   Top with marshmallows.

Dreamsicle® Cooler

1. Place in blender:
   1/3 cup Dreamsicle® Drink Mix
   8 ice cubes
   1 cup milk
2. Blend on high until ice is crushed.

Dreamsicle® Milkshake

1. Place 1 scoop soft vanilla ice cream and 1 cup
   milk into a quart jar.
2. Add 1/3 cup Dreamsicle® Mix.
3. Place lid on jar and shake until blended.

Strawberry Drink Mix

Make Dreamsicle® Drink Mix, but color the sugar red or pink with red food coloring and change the orange flavored drink mix to Strawberry Quik®.
Change the mini marshmallows to pink and white.

Cinnamon Cappuccino Mix in a Pint Jar

Ingredients for Jar

Mix next two ingredients in small bowl:

3/4 cup + 3 Tb. sugar

2 tsp. cinnamon

1/3 cup instant coffee

Mix next two ingredients in small bowl:

1/2 cup powdered sugar

1/2 cup powdered coffee creamer

Size of Jar: Pint

Place Ingredients in Jar in This Order:

(If you want to make a diagonal design read pg. 5 before putting ingredients in jar.)

1. Place cinnamon sugar mixture in jar first.
2. Place coffee in jar next, spreading coffee evenly to edges of jar.
3. Place creamer mixture into jar last.
4. Leave layered as is or make a "Sand-Art" design (pg. 5).
5. Decorate jar (pg. 4).
6. Attach recipe on pg. 27 to jar.

Victorian Baskets

Give some of these mixes in a fancy, lacy basket. Include some antique china cups and saucers (inexpensive at flea markets) and lace edged napkins.

Decorate the jar mixes with lace and satin ribbons and glue small silk flowers on top of the jars.

Use Victorian notecards or stickers to include a message, poem or the drink instructions.

This recipe continued from pg. 26.

Cinnamon Cappuccino

1. Empty cappuccino mix into a large mixing bowl.
2. Blend very well with a whisk.
3. Place mix back into jar or a container of your choice.
4. Place 1 1/2 to 2 Tb. mix into a cup. Add 1 cup boiling water. Stir until mixture is completely dissolved. Top with whipped cream if desired.

Cinnamon Cappuccino Cooler

1. Place 1 cup milk, 10 small ice cubes and 2 Tb. Cinnamon Cappuccino Mix into a blender.
2. Blend on high until ice cubes are completely crushed. Serve immediately.

Cinnamon Cappuccino Shake

1. Place 1 scoop soft vanilla ice cream and 1 cup milk into a quart jar.
2. Add 2 Tb. Cinnamon Cappuccino Mix.
3. Place lid on jar and shake until blended (or blend in a blender).

Fabrics, Ribbons and Bows

Don't limit yourself to fabric for the top of the jars. Use a paper doily, a lace handkerchief, Battenburg lace square, paper from a brown paper sack.

Ribbon choices - almost unlimited - ribbon printed with designs, multi-tone wired ribbons, sheer wired ribbons, polka-dot ribbons, striped ribbons, satin ribbons, lacy ribbons, raffia (in all colors), 2 or 3 colors of 1/8" or 1/4" wide ribbon together, shiny bright colored wires with stars attached, gingham ribbons, metallic ribbons, plaid ribbons, ribbons that say "Happy Birthday" or "Merry Christmas".

Creamy Cappuccino Mix in a Pint Jar

Flavors: Amaretto, Hazelnut, Vanilla, Mocha Almond and Irish Creme

Ingredients for Jar

Mix following 3 ingredients in a medium bowl:
1/3 cup dry milk
2/3 cup + 1 Tb. sugar
2/3 cup flavored* powdered coffee creamer

1/3 cup instant coffee

*Powdered coffee creamer is available in several flavors. Try amaretto, hazelnut, vanilla, mocha almond and Irish creme.

Size of Jar: Pint

Place Ingredients in Jar in This Order:

(If you want to make a diagonal design read pg. 5 before putting ingredients in jar.)

1. Place half the milk mixture in jar first.
2. Place coffee in jar next, spreading evenly.
3. Add remaining milk mixture.
4. Leave layered as is or make a "Sand-Art" design (pg. 5).
5. Decorate jar (pg. 4).
6. Attach recipe on pg. 29 to jar. Name coffee by flavor.

Seashells

Buy seashells at the crafts store. Hot glue one or more seashells on top of the fabric on your jar. Have everything in place and then add the shell. Coordinate the fabric and ribbon with the colors of the seashell. Seashells look good with heavy ecru lace.

This recipe continued from pg. 28.

Creamy _____Cappuccino

1. Empty Coffee Mix into a large mixing bowl.
2. Blend very well with a whisk.
3. Place mix back into the jar or into a container of your choice.
4. Place 1 1/2 to 2 Tb. mix into a cup. Add 1 cup boiling water. Stir until mixture is completely dissolved. Top with whipped cream if desired.

Personalized Mugs

Give mixes in a basket with mugs that you have bought at a discount store and personalized with DecoArt Ultra Gloss Acrylic Enamel® (craft store).

This is a paint that can be made dishwasher and microwave safe by baking the painted mug in the oven. (Instructions come on the jar of paint.)

Personalize or decorate mug with the recipient's name or write "Happy Birthday from Mary", "Merry Christmas, Grandma" or "Mom's Tea". Add a design to the mug freehand or with a stencil.

Color coordinate the mugs with the decorations on the jars of mix.

Chocolate Cinnamon Cappuccino Mix in a Pint Jar

Ingredients for Jar

Mix next two ingredients in small bowl:

3/4 cup sugar

2 tsp. cinnamon

1/4 cup cocoa powder

1/2 cup powdered sugar

1/3 cup instant coffee

1/3 cup powdered coffee creamer

Size of Jar: Pint

Place Ingredients in Jar in This Order:

(If you want to make a diagonal design read pg. 5 before putting ingredients in jar.)

1. Place cinnamon sugar mixture in jar first.
2. Place cocoa powder in jar next, spreading cocoa evenly to edges of jar. Use a paper towel to wipe inside of jar clean.
3. Place powdered sugar into jar next.
4. Place coffee into jar next, spreading coffee evenly to edges of jar.
5. Place coffee creamer into jar last.
6. Leave layered as is or make a "Sand-Art" design (pg. 5).
7. Decorate jar (pg. 4).
8. Attach recipe on pg. 31 to jar.

This recipe continued from pg. 30.

 # Chocolate Cinnamon Cappuccino

1. Empty cappuccino mix into a large mixing bowl.
2. Blend very well with a whisk.
3. Place mix back into jar or a container of your choice.
4. Place 1 1/2 Tb. mix into a cup. Add 1 cup boiling water. Stir until mixture is completely dissolved. Top with whipped cream if desired.

Chocolate Cinnamon Cappuccino Cooler

1. Place 1 cup milk, 10 small ice cubes and 1 1/2 Tb. Chocolate Cinnamon Cappuccino Mix into a blender.
2. Blend on high until ice cubes are completely crushed. Serve immediately.

Chocolate Cinnamon Cappuccino Shake

1. Place 1 scoop soft vanilla ice cream and 1 cup milk into a quart jar.
2. Add 2 Tb. Chocolate Cinnamon Cappuccino Mix.
3. Place lid on jar and shake until blended (or mix in a blender).

Stained Glass Jars

Buy some "stained glass paint" (crafts stores). Paint directly onto the jar, or paint a design onto a slick surface. let it dry well, pull it up and place it on the jar.

The design will adhere to the jar until peeled off. By using this technique you can paint on a flat horizontal surface rather than right on the jar and if you make a mistake you can start over.

Kid's Project - For Fun or Profit!

Since there is no cooking involved in making these mixes, why not cover a table in the garage with a sheet and have a group of kids (siblings, scout troop, band members, choir members) make dozens of mixes for gifts or a fund-raising project? Even young children can help. For older ones, assign someoi to sweep out the garage when finished, someone to wash the sheet, etc. Let them do the planning and the clean up.

Make these assembly line style with a table for decorating th finished jars and another table for writing the instructions.

Index